My Achilles

Stanley Iyanu

Burning Eye

BurningEyeBooks
Never Knowingly
Mainstream

This edition published by Burning Eye Books 2023

www.burningeye.co.uk

@burningeyebooks

Burning Eye Books
15 West Hill, Portishead, BS20 6LG

ISBN 978-1-913958-41-1

To Mum, my sister Ope and baby Jerry

*

Prologue

For those who are lost, who were offered on the altar,
who died a second death and bled like lambs to slaughter.
For those who drank the wine, which went down like sweet nectar,
in rooms of acrid smoke, in plumes of white and whispers.
For those who have devoured and feasted upon morsels
and yielded unto custom and saw naught in the aether.
For those who turned to conmen who tore flesh they discarded,
and hungered for their comfort and got nothing in return.
For those who still need answers when there is not a reason,
trust that we are the innocent – the beloved of the Lord.

ACHILLES

Lasagne

I. Ragù

    Like clockwork, I watch you in your sanctuary
in your crimson red; I inhale the passion and
breathe in your doctrine. Devoted, I lay
garlands at your feet. I could recite your lasagne
recipe line by line. How you'd turn to the camera
as if staring into me:

> *In making sure that*
> *the mince is cooked*
> *turn up the heat a touch*
> *allow it to sizzle*
> *soaking in its juices*
> *watch as it stiffens*

Without meaning to, you turn to me
and smiles sweetly, allowing me to rest.

II. Béchamel

    In this reflection,
shame shrouds secrecy
and seals his lips shut.
I stare as it literally embalms him.
I watch as he shrinks himself,
fades into withdrawal.
I wish I could shelter him.
Tell him to look at the
honest eyes staring back
with love and abundance.
Tell him that light shines
brightly when you let it,
when you stop howling at the moon.
Tell him that in the fullness of
himself, he is deserving of so
much more than shame.

III. *Parmigiana*

Duty is a strange creature,
how it permeates through every familial bond,
how it upholds both service and self-sacrifice,
how love is not always enough.

IV. *Buon appetito*

I delve my hands into the deep
and raise up the blade and stare
as the shine stares back at me,
scrub off each letter like a flimsy veneer
and see that it's dull and pure.
The dish brush knows the secret
shut behind hardened enamel.
The dish brush knows I'm gay,
knows how hard it is to say.

a guide to birdwatching

quietly, he drops what he can find
rustling deep in his pockets for seeds
suet sticks to his fingertips
grizzling up to him
I'm used to this:
                        straw sucking
                        leaves crunching
                        wind rustling

it's now stopped raining –
so he's off to feed the birds

watch, how they approach him
surround him, linger and chatter
adoring him more than the   morsels   he   leaves

in this moment, they need him
but I realise I need him more

Ode to Healing

inspired by characters in The Perks of Being a Wallflower

As Charlie, I lie starfish on the cold snow,
head pressed in deep, cold snaps all over,
amber noise fading into the background.
I give myself over to the numbness,
surrender to the silence, don't fight it:
how I feel both sad and happy, frozen
although very much alive.

> I save myself,
> choose myself,
> accept myself
> and stop accepting
> love I do not deserve.

As Patrick, I am purple and bruised,
face puffed up like a balloon.
In this moment, invisible to you,
the silence hits harder than fists do.
Crumpled in shapes, battered, bruised.
Perhaps terror and screams sound cool?
If he knows the truth, then who are you?
Now Charlie comes to the rescue.

> I grieve myself
> to find myself,
> question myself
> and stop accepting
> love I do not deserve.

As Sam, I embrace this heartbreak
and don a crown of least resistance,
make me infinite.
Watching you crack whips, break
hearts, remould, place plaster casts
on broken hearts, mended till they
are whole. Chipped but whole.
You want someone who is delicate

and supple, lusting after you –
until you get it.

I heal myself,
find love in myself,
rebuild myself
and stop accepting
love I do not deserve.

I don't want to be a hashtag

1: LUST [for life]
I want to feel the cool breeze on my skin,
taste the fresh air, lust for a life worth living
without fear, desire to run, buy food,
go for a drive, stay home, wear a hoodie
and not be a hashtag.

2: WRATH [anger]
I am not a human.
I am an Other,
a physical entity of black and/or brown skin.
I do not exist.
I persist in the shadows,
King Kong brute, white woman in arm.
I will burn this country down.
I will cause an outrage of fire.

3: SLOTH [apathy]
This chip cuts in deep,
scratches fibres, tears like thread,
precipitates pain in pumps of blood
that pour onto busy streets.
You watch and leave.
Wind blows black, brown bodies
motionless in the breeze
Turn off the TV.

4: GLUTTONY [binge]
Oversaturated, overindulged,
force-feed the trauma on display.
Gorge on viral triggers like feasting on hurt
till it feels normal;
click the images of brutality.
Death should not feel normal,
or to be a glutton choking on the conduct
of immoral monsters.

5: GREED [loot]
If I should die before I wake,
I pray to God my soul to take.
I ask him to set streets ablaze
till smoke and embers fill this place.
Pick and grab the goods you find.
May God have mercy on those left behind.

6: PRIDE [St George]
I live in a quintessential English countryside
where the wildlife scurries from the woods
and runs amok in open fields, green grass,
and daffodils.
I don't see race.

I live in English gentry, cream teas,
afternoon tea, fine art, and high cuisine,
where I worked for what I have
and what belongs to me,
so why are *they* looting?

I live in England, home of fish and chips,
Magna Carta, prestige, and the King.
We don't have a problem with race.
Say their name?
Say their name?
The UK is not innocent.

7: ENVY [hope]
Malcolm, Medgar, Baldwin, King.
Names of men who each had dreams.
If this life is worth living
don't die as a hashtag
but as a human being.

I Smell Like Popcorn

I remind you of a smell / resplendent / similar to your past / I remind you of the nostalgia of a sunny day pebble beach and salt & vinegar chips / I'm your afternoon treat after a trip to the pictures before a midnight boogie / I give you that warmth you need that reminder of home that sense that you are not alone / holding my hand down the winding road

You said I 'smell like popcorn' / a smell so good / a smell so inviting / popping kernels in a white flame as the oil burns / a chemical reaction takes place / this image locked in your memory / popping up / readying your path to follow as I lead you into that familiar sense of home / pretty box yours blue stripes mine has the ribbons you gave me /

If I remind you of popcorn / I remind you of a home / a home away from home / a home where you are not alone / a home where you can be at home with me / I hold you close to my memory / building sandcastles / sand grains on our palms / sand in between our toes / playing bucket and spades in the rock pools / crabs flitter by

If I smell like popcorn / then I'm your sense of home / and you / are my sunshine / and bright blue skies

PATROCLUS

The Truth About Jellyfish

There are no blank verses about you,
no sonnets or heroic couplets
to do justice to your essence,
so let this be yours and yours alone.

You float in the water,
letting the waves wash over you,
pulsating in this fantasy.
Underwater diving into the unknown,
drift away into the deep with me,
dive into this discovery,
I'll follow you down.
Shine your light and lead the way,
meet me where I am and
I'll be with you forever.

Isn't it strange that
I'm deep-sea diving with you
and I feel that the world is all right?
Dancing above the sea floor,
I'd swim through oceans
just to find you.

My eternal, my everlasting.
Time is no constraint.
Time has no power in this moment.
Take my hand and lead the way.

Sweetest Song

I run my fingers through your hair
my hand caresses your curls
wrapped around my fingertips
like strings on a guitar
your body plays the sweetest song

I hear the hum
I hear the rhythm
I hear the beat of every quake
the shockwaves of our embrace
the vibrations that you make
your eyes roll back into space
the cymbals and drumbeats
the gentle notes of your heart against mine

this percussion deserves
a rapturous applause
I am the conductor
I look into your eyes
there's a focus
there's stillness
there's a pull that draws
me closer and closer to you

follow through
sustain the echoes
hold the note
feel the rhythm
I refuse to let this music stop

the everything

my forearm is a pillow

& it's the longest
you've been still
so much so that
I miss the chaos
that frantic energy
vibrancy in your smile

& you're deep in this
silent in slumber but
loud in my thoughts
willing the noises
outside to hush so
not to wake you up

& I'm currently fixed
rest my bones against
your bones, stroke the
hair on your chest – it's
the poignance in this
the feeling of forever

& geometric shapes stir
you to sleep, the covers
wrapped so tightly you're
radiating heat; warmth
drawing in on me, I breathe
in the sweet, the still

the everything

Daisy Chain

all around is still
still in this moment
almost stagnant
like the world has frozen
in time and anything
and all that's there
is still
is at peace

lost in the garden
the sun emblazoned in the sky
warms my skin

the light-breaks disturb the quiet
stealing silence like giggles *at night*
breaking into *the hush*
waking up this still life around:
a rusting car
covered by shade and droppings
a lonely tree
a torn swing
naked

I still slumber for the stillness of birdsong
rippling through the air while
the sky is mellow
calm in its azure –
a cerulean quality

'let's play with the flowers,' you say
holding   picking any wild flowers
their   smell   enters my nostril
I taste   the tang   and roll my eyes
you start to make a daisy chain
with   the others
you look beautiful

I gave you daisies
you gave me kisses
and I begged for more
        effeuiller la marguerite
he loves me
            he loves me not
to what extent?
                un peu
beaucoup
he loves me like how the grass bends
and leans
he loves me like the tan lines scorched
on his skin
he loves me then he loves me *pas du tout*
but I am just intoxicated with you
mais je suis juste ivre de vous
tu me plais – I like you

Rolling in the Grass

I miss our voice memos
your goofy little laugh
rolling in the grass
the blades tucked in my jeans
as you kiss me softly

hidden by the shrubs
I feel the earth beneath us
and this feeling is unmatched

only soft music in the distance
I can hear it
I can feel the way
my heart beats for you
I want to stay in this moment
bathe in the happy and let the
endorphins wash over me
and make me clean

sometimes I'm struck by the work I do
too buttoned-up by policies
policies that have far too
much sway to my happy

you're a catalyst stirring up my rate of reaction
forcing the speed of things to act
a fiction needed to wake me into focus
there's life
outside office walls
outside deadlines and meetings
outside emails and bounce-backs
a tender kiss
and time stops

wipe away the fears

kiss away all doubts
this moment unmatched in my mind
delaying the time, we will depart and
say goodbye
you fed me with love
and I returned my need
my want for you
stay, my love –
if only time would freeze
here, I'd stay with you
just rolling in the grass

THESIS

Nitrogen

My mother is a hoarder,
collecting memories and moments
both mediocre and sublime.
VCR tapes wrapped in plastic
stored in large brown boxes
placed in dust – safe for time.

My mother acts like a hoarder,
holding on to the magic of simpler times.
Always during breakfast, she
turns away to tend to the pot,
sweet smell of stew
hugging the air around.

I've always loved food,
anticipating how *good* the Naija food will taste,
wondering when and *why* it's taking so long –
never realising that it takes as long as it *always* takes.

My mother became a hoarder
when Sis and I were infants and she
tried to keep the mementos of a bygone time:
how we'd play in the streets with the neighbours' kids,
cherry knocking on doors, kicking footballs,
chomping on penny sweets in white paper bags.

I now hoard memory like my mother,
clutching on to fair and foul times.
I put myself back into those clothes,
those photos, framed in time,
of sitting at the breakfast table
with food on my mind.

Little Lagos

at five I'd never seen space
that big, so vast and expansive
adorned with white plastic seats
peppered under fluorescent strobe lights
it carried the shapes of bodies dancing
Reebok trainers and alligator skin shoes
traipsing across the dance floor
and it felt like home
music resonating through the concrete
beats you felt underfoot from tunes that soared into the
night sky
Eternal, All Saints, Another Level, Cameo on the radio
the smell of jollof rice taking you by the hand, guiding
you to sit
past the mummy with her cooler container
right by the sharki and salt fish, moi moi
fruit juice for the Christians
next to the uncles on the alcohol
and the aunties on the prowl
tables stacked with Supermalt bottles
and Shloer (or *Shola*) we could not pronounce
back then, you danced and danced
until weightless, lost in slumber
now I'm thirty-*something*, awaking in a big comfy bed
remembering how it felt like home –
that it's now been demolished

Citrus Fruit

I don't like the taste of mangoes

the awkward tang and sweetness
the occasional hints of sour
where my father is from
grow trees as tall as towers
mangoes built towards the sky

I'm expected to water this plantation
tend to its overshoots and dry soil
nourish it in the back-breaking sun
to smooth over cracks and plant new life
but I could never be satisfied with its taste

my father devours the fruit
blitzes it until it is mulch
that once-glimmering mango
now nothing and no more
I still don't like the taste

weird + wonderful

you are not the boy you once were
gone are the thin legs, high ankle socks
and church clothes that no longer fit
braces have removed your gaps
so you no longer hide your smile

you are not the boy you once were
gone is the shyness, that small waist
the need for a father's love –
but thankfully so is the fear
in being who you really are

you are not the boy you once were
your innocence is a thing of the past
but your heart remains the same
that boy so gentle and tender
is a man now, weird + wonderful

the kindest of souls

Zhûnbèi
When your fists pull back to strike
ready your gaze
turn your body
into the punch
eyeward, glare
breathe, focus
your dexterity
into landing
the punch

Goan
Feel the
impact
as if
they
were
there
Sho

...then do the same with the left hand

My family
use fists
to fight, fists
to strike, break
bricks into cinder
destroy wood into planks
rolling clattered on the dojo floor
but they are the kindest of souls

My family
assault air
with high kicks
back kicks, jumping
turning kicks, piercing the
atmosphere climbing feet-first high
then touch the ground to repeat

but they are the kindest of souls

My family
wield weapons
armoury dull but dangerous in hand
practise kicks to break bones, pull back
strikes able to shatter a sacrum or two
then talk about DnD or Marvel movies

Nerds with black belts to the nth degree and they are the
kindest of souls

Attention

Bow

HECTOR

Dandelion in the Wind

let's speak in the morning
and let the misunderstanding
grow within the cracks between us

when you sleep next to me
I can hear the unsettled
frustration when you breathe
there's no comfort in those sighs
a coldness in your turning

come closer is what I am thinking
but those words I will not say
you will be gone in the morning and
I now just wait for you to leave
though every part of me
hopes that you will stay
because that's what you want
but at the table
the coffee has gone cold
your seat unused
toast unfinished
the radio is mocking me
your presence is gone and I miss it terribly

replaying everything the morning after
wondering if this is a conversation
I should be having with you
wondering if *I'm sorry* or
it'll be all right or
let's speak in the morning
was such a good idea

I would go back in time
but I wonder if this would
always   be the outcome
your love is a dandelion
about to blow in the wind
swaying each way
floating by
far   far   far
away from me
and I am the wind
that's pushing you away
but never pulling you back.

Medusa

If I am a monster, then let me show you:
how I'd glisten in the moonlight,
the last sight you'd see. What? Tusks?
No, cold frigid rock, fixed in stone.

If I could cry, I'd fill the earth with tears;
valleys would flow from ducts, water would
form springs, or oceans, endless leagues
surrounding you, with no land to escape.

If my anger could speak, those gods would not save you
from my wrath. The Scylla or Charybdis would rip
you to shreds on my command. I'd call all sea life to battle
and launch them straight to your kingdom.

If I stopped to feel, then I'd be turned to stone,
left to deal with what he's done, made to grieve
from her words. Or by the lack of choice in this,
the so-called punishment or supposed protection.

If I had choice in any of this, I'd burn the pages,
singe the work of poets to dust and scorch the
Greek and accompanying syntax. Tell them to write
no more lies, tell them to make me even more ferocious. So
that

if I dance, it will be on your rocky carcass, grind
your face straight to the ground. Reduce your
core to powder, sprinkle it into the Aegean,
then blow you into the wind.

Atlas

I stop the blood and
tell him that in his mouth is
where a universe can be found
a galaxy on his tongue

that in this present, we are limitless
like shooting stars spinning so bright
the space between us, now, so vast
so wholly dense with silence
it feels expansive and lonely

in his arms, I held warmth
as if the sun shrank inward
and seeped into his palms
his whole being, light rays of calm

and now with reddened eyes
I call him Ganesh and ask him
to permit me into his personal cosmos
remove all asteroids and obstacles on our path
destroy every impediment and stay here

I drop the heavens he promised me
and let go of this burden – no more Atlas
as the sky droops so heavy over us
until it ebbs and flows into the void

I stopped the blood
and still lost him

Space Dust

clumps of matter in the distance
forms of beings too far to see
I search for you in vacant places
but it's not you I see

you're off in outer space
and I can't find you
missing the cluster of stars
that once were
that formed you
the ghost of a being
now gone

the cold reminds me
that nothing or no one is missing
that nobody is coming
the constellations form into a semblance of you

      the northern sky bears Andromeda
      mirrors this sense of longing
      if Perseus came down, he'd break down the chains
      and fetters that bound you in place – on winged feet
      letting time no longer delay
      the hours would be telescopes
      the moon, an oracle
      to show me where he is and come find us,   finally

Nothing

you and I are dust storms
under a cloudless sky
the stars watch
violent, heady rage
colliding with cold, frigid air
until there is nothing

into the vast unknown
the sky glows incandescent with rage
sparking a viciousness into the air
red, azure hues bleed across said sky
illuminating nothing

in the sobering moments before and after
hold me like nothing has gone on
hold me like nothing is wrong with us
hold me

Milton Keynes UK
Ingram Content Group UK Ltd.
UKHW011817061023
430090UK00004B/46

9 781913 958411